OUR LIVING WORLD

Spiders

By **Jenny Tesar**

With Illustrations by Robert Clement Kray

Series Editor: Vincent Marteka
Introduction by John Behler, *New York Zoological Society*

A BLACKBIRCH PRESS BOOK

WOODBRIDGE, CONNECTICUT

Published by Blackbirch Press, Inc.
One Bradley Road, Suite 205
Woodbridge, CT 06525

Printed in Canada

10 9 8 7 6 5 4 3 2 1

Editorial Director: Bruce Glassman
Editor: Geraldine C. Fox
Editorial Assistant: Michelle Spinelli
Design Director: Sonja Kalter
Production: Sandra Burr, Rudy Raccio

Library of Congress Cataloging-in-Publication Data

Tesar, Jenny E.
    Spiders / by Jenny Tesar: introduction by John Behler—1st ed.
       p.   cm. — (Our living world)
    Includes bibliographical references and index.
    Summary: Explores the physical characteristics, senses, metabolism, reproduction, and growth of spiders.
    ISBN 1-56711-043-6   ISBN 1-56711-062-2 (Trade)
    1. Spiders—Juvenile literature. [1. Spiders.] I. Title. II. Series.
QL458.4.T47   1993
595.4'4—dc20   93-10446
                                                            CIP
                                                             AC

Contents

What Does It Mean to Be "Alive"?

Introduction by John Behler,
New York Zoological Society

One summer morning, as I was walking through a beautiful field, I was inspired to think about what it really means to be "alive." Part of the answer, I came to realize, was right in front of my eyes.

The meadow was ablaze with color, packed with wildflowers at the height of their blooming season. A multitude of insects, warmed by the sun's early-morning rays, began to stir. Painted turtles sunned themselves on an old mossy log in a nearby pond. A pair of wood ducks whistled a call as they flew overhead, resting near a shagbark hickory on the other side of the pond.

As I wandered through this unspoiled habitat, I paused at a patch of milkweed to look for monarch-butterfly caterpillars, which depend on the milkweed's leaves for food. Indeed, the caterpillars were there, munching away. Soon these larvae would spin their cocoons, emerge as beautiful orange-and-black butterflies, and begin a fantastic 1,500-mile (2,400-kilometer) migration to wintering grounds in Mexico. It took biologists nearly one hundred years to unravel the life history of these butterflies. Watching them in the milkweed patch made me wonder how much more there is to know about these insects and all the other living organisms in just that one meadow.

The patterns of the natural world have often been likened to a spider's web, and for good reason. All life on Earth is interconnected in an elegant yet surprisingly simple design, and each living thing is an essential part of that design. To understand biology and the functions of living things, biologists have spent a lot of time looking at the differences among organisms. But in order to understand the very nature of living things, we must first understand what they have in common.

The butterfly larvae and the milkweed—and all animals and plants, for that matter—are made up of the same basic elements. These elements are obtained, used, and eliminated by every living thing in a series of chemical activities called metabolism.

Every molecule of every living tissue must contain carbon. During photosynthesis, green plants take in carbon dioxide from the atmosphere. Within their chlorophyll-filled leaves, in the presence of sunlight, the carbon dioxide is combined with water to form sugar—nature's most basic food. Animals need carbon, too. To grow and function, animals must eat plants or other animals that have fed on plants in order to obtain carbon. When plants and animals die, bacteria and fungi help to break down their tissues. This allows the carbon in plants and animals to be recycled. Indeed, the carbon in your body—and everyone else's body—may once have been inside a dinosaur, a giant redwood, or a monarch butterfly!

All life also needs nitrogen. Nitrogen is an essential component of protoplasm, the complex of chemicals that makes up living cells. Animals acquire nitrogen in the same manner as they acquire carbon dioxide: by eating plants or other animals that have eaten plants. Plants, however, must rely on nitrogen-fixing bacteria in the soil to absorb nitrogen from the atmosphere and convert it into proteins. These proteins are then absorbed from the soil by plant roots.

Living things start life as a single cell. The process by which cells grow and reproduce to become a specific organism—whether the organism is an oak tree or a whale—is controlled by two basic substances called deoxyribonucleic acid (DNA) and ribonucleic acid (RNA). These two chemicals are the building blocks of genes that determine how an organism looks, grows, and functions. Each organism has a unique pattern of DNA and RNA in its genes. This pattern determines all the characteristics of a living thing. Each species passes its unique pattern from generation to generation. Over many billions of years, a process involving genetic mutation and natural selection has allowed species to adapt to a constantly changing environment by evolving—changing genetic patterns. The living creatures we know today are the results of these adaptations.

Reproduction and growth are important to every species, since these are the processes by which new members of a species are created. If a species cannot reproduce and adapt, or if it cannot reproduce fast enough to replace those members that die, it will become extinct (no longer exist).

In recent years, biologists have learned a great deal about how living things function. But there is still much to learn about nature. With high-technology equipment and new information, exciting discoveries are being made every day. New insights and theories quickly make many biology textbooks obsolete. One thing, however, will forever remain certain: As living things, we share an amazing number of characteristics with other forms of life. As animals, our survival depends upon the food and functions provided by other animals and plants. As humans—who can understand the similarities and interdependence among living things—we cannot help but feel connected to the natural world, and we cannot forget our responsibility to protect it. It is only through looking at, and understanding, the rest of the natural world that we can truly appreciate what it means to be "alive."

1

Spiders:
The Overview

Remember the last time you took a walk through a field of grass? How many spiders did you see along the way? Perhaps you didn't see any spiders at all, but they were there.

How many spiders did you see in your home today? Perhaps none, but they are there, too.

Spiders are very common creatures. They live almost everywhere on Earth. Once when people counted the number of spiders in a grassy field in England, they found that there were more than 2 million spiders in 1 acre (0.4 hectare)!

Spiders are found in deserts, high mountains, grasslands, marshes, and forests. Some live in caves; others live on beaches. Many kinds of spiders live in people's homes and gardens. There is even a spider that spends its entire life underwater.

Opposite:
Spiders inhabit almost every kind of environment on Earth. Here, a colorful orb-weaving spider sits on its web.

The Body of a Spider

Some people confuse spiders with insects. Both spiders and insects belong to a large group of animals known as arthropods. Arthropods are invertebrates (animals without backbones) with jointed legs and a tough outer skeleton. The skeleton, called the exoskeleton, is like a suit of armor. It protects the soft body parts from disease and from drying out. Muscles are attached to the inner surface of the exoskeleton.

An insect's body is divided into three parts: head, thorax, and abdomen. A spider's body has only two parts. The front part is a combined head-and-thorax region called the cephalothorax. This name comes from the Greek words for *head* and *chest*. The back part of a spider's body is the abdomen. It is connected to the cephalothorax by a narrow waist.

The cephalothorax is covered by a large, hard shield called the carapace. At the front end of the

A Leg Up

Each of your legs has two basic segments, the thigh and the calf, which are separated by a joint called the knee. A spider's leg has seven segments that are separated by joints. Since a spider's legs have so many joints, they are much more flexible than yours.

The External Anatomy of a Spider

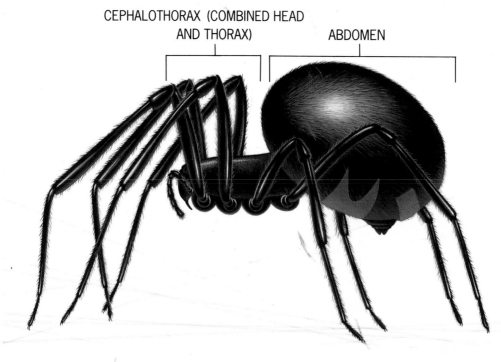

CEPHALOTHORAX (COMBINED HEAD AND THORAX)   ABDOMEN

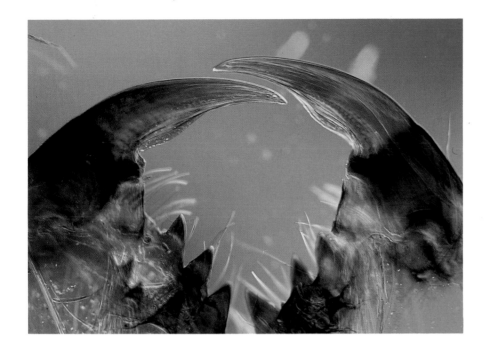

An enlarged photo shows the poison fangs of the epcira spider. On each spider's chelicera is a sharp, movable fang that is used to stab prey. Venom from a spider's poison glands flows through tiny tubes in the chelicerae and out the openings in the fangs.

carapace are the eyes. Most spiders have eight simple eyes. Insects usually have five eyes: two large compound eyes and three simple eyes. Insects also have antennae, or feelers, on their heads; spiders do not have antennae.

Perhaps the easiest way to tell the difference between a spider and an insect is to count the legs. Spiders have four pairs of legs. Insects have three pairs. And spiders, unlike insects, have no wings.

In addition to four pairs of legs, spiders have two other pairs of appendages. In front of a spider's mouth is a pair of jaws called chelicerae. Each chelicera has two segments: a stout base and a sharp, movable fang. The spider uses its fangs to stab the bodies of prey (the animals it eats). Near the end of each fang is a tiny opening. Venom from poison glands flows through tubes in the chelicerae and out the openings, into the prey.

On each side of the mouth is a small appendage called a pedipalp. The pedipalps look like little legs and are used in eating. In male spiders, they are also important for reproduction.

Waist Control

Spiders aren't the only animals with eight legs. Their closest relatives in the animal kingdom also have eight legs. These relatives include scorpions, mites, ticks, and daddy longlegs (which are different from daddy-longlegs spiders). One way to distinguish a spider from its relatives is to look at its midsection. A narrow waist connects the spider's cephalothorax to its abdomen. The spider's relatives do not have waists.

Weave It to a Spider

Some kinds of behavior are learned, but other kinds do not need to be learned. Non-learned behaviors are referred to as inborn behaviors. A shamrock spider, for example, is not taught how to make a web. It is born with this knowledge. It weaves webs, using the same techniques that shamrock spiders have always used. But the webs of one shamrock spider may not look exactly like the webs of other shamrock spiders. A spider's webs are as unique as human fingerprints.

Silk Makers

Every spider has silk glands in its abdomen. The glands produce liquid silk, which is similar to a substance found in human hair. The liquid silk is squeezed out of the body through tiny holes in finger-like appendages near the rear of the abdomen called spinnerets (spinning organs). As soon as the liquid silk is exposed to air, it hardens, forming a thread. The thread may be only one millionth of an inch in diameter.

Some spiders have as many as five kinds of silk glands. Different kinds of glands produce different kinds of silk. Some silk threads are very strong—stronger perhaps than steel threads of the same diameter. Others are elastic and can stretch like rubber bands. They do not break when an insect crashes into them. One kind of silk reflects ultraviolet light. Humans cannot see ultraviolet light, but many insects are attracted to it.

Every spider has silk glands that produce liquid silk. The silk is squeezed out of the body through tiny holes in the abdomen called spinnerets. When the liquid silk comes into contact with the air, it gels and forms a thread.

How an Orb Web is Built

Eager Weavers

A spider may use its web as a home, as a place to catch prey, and as a place to meet a mate and raise its young. Webs used to catch prey often have two kinds of threads—some are made of dry silk, and others are made of sticky silk. The spider knows which threads are which—that's why a spider is never trapped in its own web!

Not all spiders weave webs. Those that do, use a wide range of designs. Each design is an adaptation to its owner's environment and needs. Here are a few examples of web-spinning spiders and their webs:

Orb weavers make the most beautiful webs. They look like pinwheels and have many spiral turns crossed by radii, or spokes, that meet in the center. At each point where a radius crosses the spiral, the spider uses a drop of sticky mucus to glue the threads together. This makes the web strong but flexible. In an average-size orb web, the spiral is connected to radii at more than 1,000 points!

Tangled-web spiders make tangled, messy-looking webs. These webs are attached to branches and other supports by long threads. Tangled-web spiders often live in cellars and other dark places in people's homes. Their old, abandoned webs become covered with dust, forming what we know as familiar cobwebs.

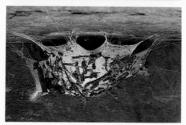

Purse-web spiders weave nets shaped like tubes. A tube is actually an extension of the spider's burrow in the ground. The spider weaves the tube up the side of a tree and, when an insect or other possible meal crawls over the tube, the spider bites it through the silk.

Sheet-web spiders weave broad, two-dimensional webs with threads that do not seem to be laid out in a pattern. Many a sheet-web spider makes its web in grass or close to the ground. Underneath, the spider weaves a small funnel-like tube and waits in the funnel for an insect to become caught in the web.

Ogre-faced spiders weave rectangular webs about the size of postage stamps. An ogre-faced spider holds its web with the ends of its front legs until it spies an approaching insect. Then the spider stretches the web wide and throws it over the insect.

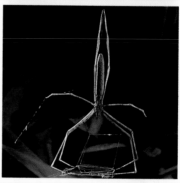

Spiders use their silk to wrap up their prey. Here, an argiope spider spins a casing around a recently trapped cricket.

Silk has many uses. Spiders use it to build webs, wrap up prey, protect eggs, and make nurseries for their babies. Another important use is to form the dragline, which is a strong double thread that a spider forms whenever it is on the move.

The dragline is really a safety line. As a spider crawls along, it glues its dragline to the surface every so often. When something frightens a spider, it seems to suddenly disappear. Actually, it lets go of the branch or other surface on which it was crawling, falls off, and hangs from its dragline until the danger passes. Then it climbs back up the dragline. When the spider is ready to return to its home, it retraces its steps, using the anchored dragline as its guide—much in the same way that people use ropes when exploring deep caves.

Silk threads are also needed for an activity called ballooning, which is used by young spiders as they travel to new homes. Soon after a spider is hatched, it crawls to the top of a twig, grass stem, or other object.

DID YOU KNOW

Never Kid an Arachnid

Most people think scorpions and daddy longlegs are spiders, but they're not. Although they are arachnids—like spiders—they do not have a waist that connects their cephalothorax to their abdomen. The sun spider is another arachnid in disguise. It has pedipalps and chelicerae, just like its close relatives, but it has only two eyes, not the eight eyes that most spiders have.

It faces the breeze, stands on the tips of its feet, and points its abdomen toward the sky. Streams of silk are released by the spinnerets. The silk threads rise into the air, pulling the spider upward. The spider drifts through the air, carried by the breeze to a new home.

Most older spiders cannot balloon, because they are too heavy. While young spiders can cover great distances by ballooning, they have no control over where breezes carry them. Many die because they are blown out to sea or dropped into other unsuitable places for spiders to live.

The Amazing Variety of Spiders

Spiders have existed for at least 380 million years. There were spiders on Earth long before humans and other vertebrates (animals with backbones). Many kinds, or species, of ancient spiders no longer exist (they are extinct). We know about these spiders because scientists have studied the remains of their bodies, which have formed fossils in rocks.

About 35,000 different species of living spiders have been identified by scientists. The actual number of species is probably much greater, but many species have not yet been identified, because lots of spiders are very tiny and easy to overlook. Some live in the ground or in other hidden places; others live in tropical forests or habitats that have not been well explored by humans.

Spiders come in many sizes. The largest are the tarantulas that live in the jungles of South America. Some weigh 4 ounces (113 grams) and have a leg span of more than 10 inches (25 centimeters); that's almost as long as this page! People call tarantulas bird spiders because they are big enough to catch and to feed on birds—as well as lizards and even small snakes!

At the other extreme are some garden spiders that are no bigger than a pinhead. Even though they are very tiny, they have eight legs and all the other body parts typical of spiders.

DID YOU KNOW

The Dance of the Spiders

There is a very lively Italian folk dance that gets its name from one type of wolf spider, the tarantula, found around the southern Italian city of Taranto. According to legend, the bite of this tarantula caused a nervous disorder that made its victims want to leap and dance. The dance, known as the tarantella, supposedly cured the condition.

Species Specifics

Tarantula

Tarantulas are big, hairy spiders. Many different kinds of spiders are called tarantulas. In the United States alone, there are about 30 species of tarantulas. Most live in the Southwest and are very different from tarantulas that live in Italy and other Mediterranean countries.

Each species of tarantula—just like all other animal species—has its own scientific name. This name is the same all over the world. Each name has two parts and is based on Greek and Latin words. For example, one U.S. tarantula is *Aphonopelma chalcodes*. The European tarantula is actually a kind of wolf spider called *Lycosa tarantula*.

When people from the United States and another country get together to talk about tarantulas, they use the scientific names. That way, everyone knows which tarantula is being discussed.

2

The Senses:
How Spiders React

A trap-door spider may spend its entire life inside its cozy, silk-lined burrow, which is covered by a door made of silk and dirt. During the day, while the spider rests, the trapdoor is closed. As darkness falls, the spider gently raises the trapdoor. Then it waits. Suddenly, it may sense the movement of a beetle. As the beetle draws near, the spider moves with lightning speed, grabbing the beetle, then killing it with injections of poison.

Like all other living things, spiders depend on their senses for learning about their environment. The senses help animals catch prey, avoid enemies, meet mates, find their way, judge distances, taste food—indeed, gather every kind of information about the environment that they need in order to survive.

A spider's senses are very different from human senses, but like human senses, they send messages to

Opposite:
A trap-door spider emerges from its hideout in pursuit of its prey. Like all other living things, spiders rely on their senses to react to their environment.

the body's nervous system. The main organ of a spider's nervous system is the brain, which is located in the cephalothorax. Nerve fibers from the brain run throughout a spider's body, carrying information to and from the brain.

When a spider senses a change in its environment, this information is relayed along nerve fibers that connect the sense organs to the brain. The brain then responds by sending a signal to another part of the body. For example, when a trap-door spider's sense organs signal the brain that a beetle is approaching, the brain signals muscles in the spider's front legs. This causes the legs to grab the beetle. The entire process takes only a fraction of a second.

How Spiders See

Most species of spiders have eight eyes, which are set in two rows. Some species have only six eyes, and others have even fewer. A species that lives in the jungles of Panama has just one eye—right in the middle of its head.

A zebra spider can jump skillfully through the air. Its quickness and agility allow it to react instantly to possible danger or a potential meal.

Old Eight Eyes

Most spiders, like this garden spider, have eight eyes. Six eyes face forward, while two eyes face off to the sides. This provides the garden spider with a wide range of vision, important because it is a hunter rather than a web-spinner. Good eyesight is essential for hunting, tracking, and waiting in ambush for prey.

In general, spiders do not have very good eyesight. For wolf spiders, jumping spiders, and several other groups, however, sight is a very important sense. These spiders do not build webs. Instead, they are hunters that track down prey or wait in ambush.

A wolf spider has a row of four small eyes just above its jaws. A little higher up there are two much bigger eyes. All six of these eyes face forward. Above the big eyes are two more big eyes, which point toward the sides. This gives the wolf spider a wide range of vision, helping it to spot movement of prey in almost any direction.

A jumping spider also has eight eyes, but they are arranged differently from those of the wolf spider. A jumping spider has two big eyes on the front of the face and one small eye on each side of the face. Above, there is a very tiny pair of eyes. Finally, near the top of the head, are two eyes that point upward. These eyes can form sharp images of objects that are as much as 12 inches (30 centimeters) away. That's a very long distance for a creature that's only 1/2 inch (1.3 centimeters) long!

Wolf spiders and jumping spiders also depend on eyesight during courtship. A male waves his legs in the air as he does an elaborate dance to attract a female. Each species has its own distinctive dance, which helps the spider recognize an appropriate mate.

The Sense of Touch

A spider's sense of touch is its most well-developed sense. It is centered in the thick coat of hairs and spines that cover a spider's body. Many of the hairs and spines are extremely sensitive to touch and to vibrations of the air, ground, or even water. As soon as something causes a hair to move, the movement is sensed by nerve endings at the base of the hair.

DID YOU KNOW

Leapers, Creepers

Human athletes who specialize in the long jump are no match for jumping spiders. A jumping spider can leap 40 times its own length! But it anchors its dragline before taking off—just in case it misses its target.

The Senses: How Spiders React

Fisher spiders live on the shores of lakes and in swamps. One species often spends the day sitting on a floating leaf, with its front legs touching the water. When a tiny fish swims nearby or an insect falls onto the water, the fisher spider senses the vibrations in the water created by the moving animal. The spider then dives into the water and grabs the prey.

Some spiders skillfully use their sense of touch to capture their prey. The fishing spider often spends its days sitting with some of its legs touching the water. When another animal swims by, the spider senses the vibrations in the water and then dives in to catch its prey.

How Spiders Hear

A spider does not hear in the way other animals do. It senses vibrations by means of lyriform organs, much in the way human eardrums pick up vibrations. Lyriform organs are a series of slit-like structures in the exoskeleton. Some of the slits occur singly; others

Because certain cave spiders are blind, they rely mostly on their sense of touch for survival. Their long legs act as antennae that sense the movements and conditions of their surroundings.

are arranged in groups. One spider may have as many as 3,000 slits on its body and legs, but most are located near the leg joints.

Inside each slit is a thin membrane (layer of animal tissue) attached to the ends of nerve cells. These cells detect forces such as vibrations that push against the membrane. For example, when an insect walks along the ground or onto a spiderweb, it creates vibrations as it moves. These vibrations are sensed by the spider's lyriform organs which, in turn, signal the nervous system to act in response.

The Senses of Taste and Smell

You taste with your tongue and smell with your nose, but a spider has neither a tongue nor a nose. The important functions of taste and smell are carried out by a spider's feet. This may seem odd to you, but the spider's feet are just as effective for tasting and smell-ing as your tongue and nose.

The end segment of a spider's leg is called the tarsus. Each tarsus has several small holes in the exoskeleton, and each hole has a sensory structure called a tarsal organ. When a spider steps into liquid, some of the liquid comes in contact with its tarsal organs. Odors from the liquid may also be detected by the tarsal organs. The nervous system identifies the chemicals in the liquid and lets the spider know if the liquid is good to drink.

An experiment once showed just how important tarsal organs can be in finding food and drink. When a scientist placed a drop of water on a front leg of a spider, the spider stepped forward to drink. When a drop was placed on a back leg, the spider turned around and drank.

Smell is also important for finding mates. There is some evidence that female tarantulas produce a chemical to attract males. A male who senses this perfume "follows his feet" to the female's burrow and begins to shake a pair of legs. This shaking causes vibrations in the ground, which are sensed by the female. If she is interested in mating, she responds by tapping her legs on her burrow.

Spiders, unlike humans, taste by sensing odors with tarsal organs in their feet. A spider needs to step into a liquid in order to taste it and to tell if it is a suitable source of food.

3

Metabolism: How Spiders Function

Argiope is a very busy little creature. This common garden spider can often be seen moving back and forth on its web, mending areas damaged by prey or bad weather. Then argiope hangs head down in the center of its web, waiting for a new victim to land. If something disturbs it, the spider drops to the ground on a dragline. When danger passes, argiope climbs back up to its web and resumes its wait.

Each of these activities requires considerable energy. Spiders—like all other living things—get the energy that they need from food. Obtaining food, digesting it, and breaking it down for energy are processes involving a number of chemical reactions. Together, these activities are called metabolism.

Metabolism is one process that distinguishes living things from non-living ones. As long as metabolism functions properly, an organism is healthy. It grows, reproduces, and reacts to changes in its environment. When metabolism stops, an organism dies.

Opposite:
Spiders, like all other living things, get the energy they need from food. Here, a golden argiope garden spider inspects its prey—a butterfly that has been caught in its web.

What Spiders Eat

Without food, a living thing will starve to death. All spiders are carnivores; that is, they eat other animals. Most of them eat insects, a few eat other spiders, and some large tropical spiders catch mice and other small vertebrates.

Each species has its own methods of capturing prey. Some spiders lie in ambush, waiting for insects to come near. Crab spiders are ambushers; they hide in flowers, waiting for bees and wasps to come in search of nectar. Other spiders, such as wolf spiders and fisher spiders, are hunters. They are fast-moving spiders that chase down prey.

Different spiders have different methods of capturing their prey. The jumping spider, for example, hides inside flowers and waits to ambush insects as they land.

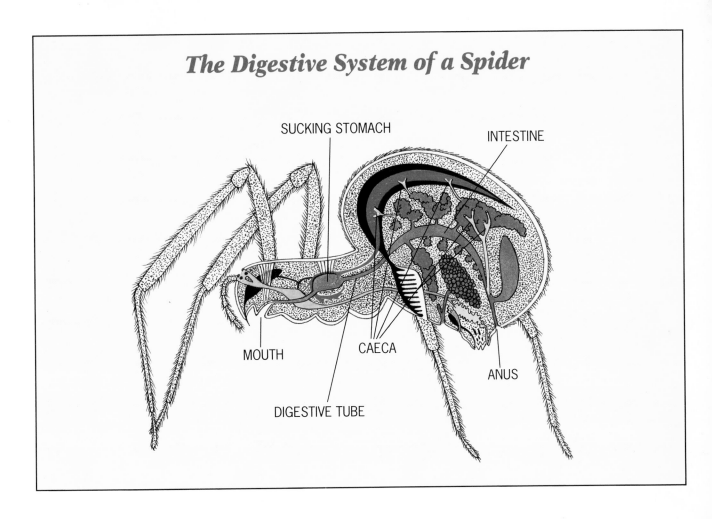

The Digestive System of a Spider

SUCKING STOMACH

INTESTINE

MOUTH

CAECA

ANUS

DIGESTIVE TUBE

Most spiders are not fussy about what they eat. They'll eat anything of the right size that lands in their web or wanders near enough to catch. It is important to a spider that food doesn't escape, so most spiders quickly inject venom into their prey. Spider venom is produced in poison glands and empties through ducts in the spider's fangs. The venom paralyzes or kills the victim.

Digesting Food

Before food can be used by the cells that make up the body of a living organism, it must be broken down into simpler forms. This process is called digestion; it takes places in the digestive system. The digestive system of a spider—like that of a human—is basically a tube that begins at the mouth and ends at the anus.

Don't Myth the Point

Many Native American myths and legends reflect the great respect that Indians have for spiders. In Pueblo folklore, it was a spider that created the first man and the first woman. In Cherokee legend, a tiny spider brought the gift of fire to other animals. The Dakotah Indians believe that a perfect orb web symbolizes the beauty of the heavens.

A spider's mouth is very small and contains no teeth. A spider cannot take in solid food; it can take in liquids only. After a spider has subdued a victim with its poison, it releases digestive juices into the animal. These juices break down the animal's soft insides, turning them into a soupy liquid.

The spider then sucks up the liquid, much in the same way that you would suck a milk shake through a straw. However, you use muscles in your lips to suck—the spider uses stomach muscles. As the powerful muscles contract, the liquid food is pulled into the stomach. It takes a common garden spider several hours to liquefy and suck up a fly. It takes a large tarantula about a day and a half to liquefy and suck up the insides of a mouse. At the end of that time, all that remains of the mouse is a little pile of fur and bones.

Further digestion takes place in the stomach and the intestine. Once digestion has been completed, the digested food passes through the wall of the intestine

Because spiders have no teeth, they must suck up all their food as liquid. Here, a wolf spider injects its digestive juices into a captured fly.

A raft spider pulls a captured minnow up onto the bank of a stream before eating it. Some spiders can kill prey much larger than themselves.

into the blood, which carries it to all parts of the spider's body. Any particles that cannot be digested then pass to the end of the intestine and out through the anus.

Attached to the digestive tube are five pairs of finger-shaped pouches called caeca. Excess food is stored in the caeca. When food is plentiful, spiders feed often. When food is scarce, spiders can use the stored food in their caeca, which makes it possible for them to go for long periods without eating.

Getting Oxygen

To produce energy from digested food, living cells need oxygen, which is obtained from the air. Most animals have special breathing mechanisms that allow them to obtain air. Spiders have two kinds of breathing systems: book lungs and tracheae. Some spiders have both systems; other species have either lungs or tracheae.

The Respiratory System of a Spider

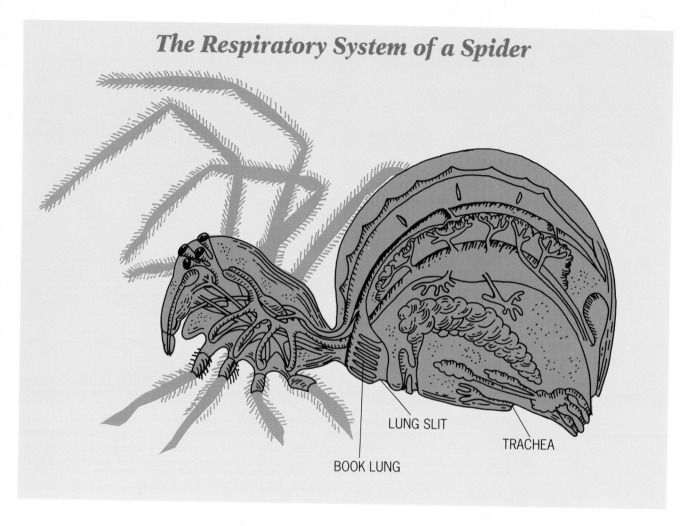

LUNG SLIT

TRACHEA

BOOK LUNG

Book lungs are gill-like structures found only in spiders and other arachnids. Scientists probably gave the organs this name because they are arranged like pages in a book. Each book lung is a hollow cavity filled with many thin, hollow plates. It is connected to the outside through an opening on the lower side of the abdomen called a lung slit.

Book lungs work much like your lungs. The plates are filled with tiny blood vessels, and air entering the book lungs moves between the plates. Oxygen from the air passes through the walls of the plates and then into the blood, which carries the oxygen throughout the spider's body.

Tracheae are thin tubes in the abdomen. They open to the outside through little holes. Air enters

Metabolism: How Spiders Function

A No-Trouble Bubble

The water spider is well named. Although it breathes air, it lives underwater—sometimes for months at a time. It hunts, feeds, mates, gives birth, and even builds webs underwater!

This spider, which lives in Europe and Asia, is about 1/2 inch (1.3 centimeters) long. It inhabits ponds and small rivers that have a lot of plant life. It is also a very good swimmer. It is active mainly at night, when it hunts for the small fishes and water insects that make up its diet.

The water spider weaves a sheet-like web of silk, which it attaches to plants that live underwater. Then it swims to the water's surface, lifts up its abdomen, and traps a tiny bubble of air under its body. Using the hairs on its back legs to hold the bubble, the spider swims back down to the web, where it releases the air bubble underneath the web. The web acts like a roof, preventing the air from rising to the surface.

The spider repeats this process a half-dozen times or more, until the bubble is large enough to be a cozy home. When necessary, the spider returns to the surface to trap more air so that its home always contains enough oxygen for breathing.

As the water spider sits in its home, its legs stick out of the bubble. Sense organs on the legs detect vibrations in the water—such as those made by an insect that has landed on the surface. When the water spider detects the nearby presence of prey, it leaves its home, taking along a tiny bubble of air attached to its abdomen. The spider pounces on its prey and injects venom into the body. Then, holding the victim with its legs and fangs, the water spider returns to its home to feed.

When mating time comes, a male water spider builds a bubble home next to the home of a female. Then he builds a silk tunnel between the two bubbles. After mating, the female lays about 50 eggs in the upper part of her bubble. The eggs hatch in about three weeks. Baby water spiders are expert swimmers. They leave their mother's home almost right away to build homes of their own.

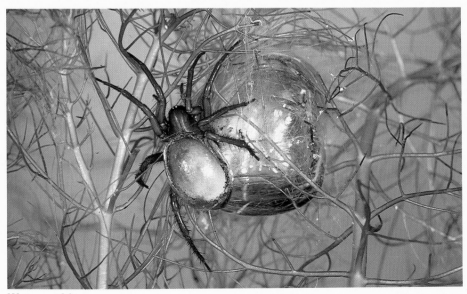

Water spider

Tracheae Tricks

The tracheae of a spider are similar to the tracheae of an insect. But insect tracheae are found throughout the entire body of the insect—even in its wings. Spider tracheae are found only in the abdomen.

You also have a trachea—it's your windpipe. Your trachea is very different from the tracheae of spiders and insects. Your trachea connects to tubes that enter your lungs, which absorb oxygen from the air. This oxygen passes into your blood, which then distributes the oxygen to all the cells in your body. Spider and insect tracheae distribute oxygen directly to cells.

through the holes and moves slowly through the tracheae. Oxygen in the air passes from the tracheae directly into cells. The blood does not play a part in distributing the oxygen, as it does in book lungs.

Removing Wastes

During metabolism, wastes are produced and have to be removed from the body. The process of removing wastes is called excretion. One of the wastes produced is carbon dioxide gas, which is excreted from a spider's body through the tracheae and book lungs.

Additional wastes, such as water and salts, are eliminated through structures called Malpighian tubules and coxal glands. Malpighian tubules are located in the spider's abdomen and function somewhat like your kidneys. The wastes collected by the tubules empty into the intestine and pass out of the spider's body through the anus.

Coxal glands are located in the lower part of the cephalothorax. They empty wastes through ducts that open between the legs.

Spider Blood

The system that moves blood through a body is called the circulatory system. Its main functions include carrying food from the intestine to the cells, and wastes from the cells to the excretory organs. Most animals have circulatory systems.

In both the spider's body and the human body, the circulatory system is made up of a heart, blood, and blood vessels. The two systems are very different. In the human body, blood always flows through blood vessels. In the spider's body, blood flows out of the blood vessels.

A spider's heart is a long, muscular tube that is located in the upper part of the animal's abdomen.

The Circulatory System of a Spider

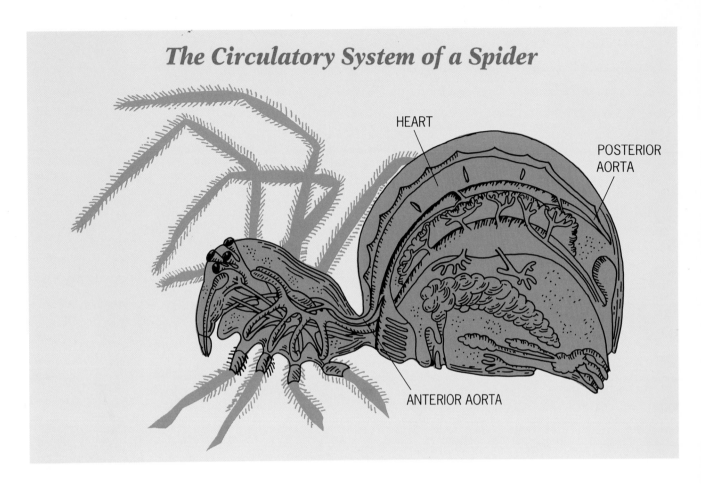

HEART

POSTERIOR AORTA

ANTERIOR AORTA

A thick blood vessel called an artery extends backward from the spider's heart, and a second large artery extends forward. Within the heart itself there are three pairs of openings.

As the heart muscles of the spider contract, blood is pumped into the animal's arteries. The blood then flows out of the arteries into spaces around the stomach, the eyes, the poison glands, and other organs. It also passes through the book lungs. Then the blood returns to the heart, entering through the three pairs of openings.

Spider blood is pale blue. The color comes from a chemical called hemocyanin, which carries oxygen throughout the spider's body—just as hemoglobin in your blood carries oxygen. However, the spider's hemocyanin is dissolved in the liquid blood. Human hemoglobin is inside blood cells.

DID YOU KNOW

Spidery Species

What do spider monkeys, spider crabs, and spider plants have in common? All were named after spiders! Spider monkeys have long, "spidery" legs, as do spider crabs, and spider plants have long, narrow leaves.

These organisms are similar in other ways, too. Like all other living things, they are made up of cells and need energy to survive. They also digest food, take in oxygen, and rid their bodies of wastes.

Metabolism: How Spiders Function

Reproduction and Growth

4

The world's living things are distinguished from non-living things in a number of ways. One of the most important differences is the ability of living things to reproduce—to create more organisms of the same kind. Creating more organisms keeps the species in existence.

Every organism has a limited life span, which means that it will eventually die. Reproduction isn't necessary to the individual organism's survival, but it is necessary to the survival of its species. The species would become extinct if its members did not reproduce enough to make up for those members lost to death.

There are two basic kinds of reproduction in the living world. In sexual reproduction, two parents are involved—a female who produces eggs and a male who produces sperm. Asexual reproduction involves only one parent; there are no eggs or sperm. Spiders,

Opposite:
Newborn house spiders scramble along some silken nest strands.

Female Kills Spiderman

Did you ever wonder how the black widow spider got its name? The female, which is much larger than the male, sometimes kills her mate. Since her "husband" is dead, she becomes a widow. And she's a black widow, not because she's in mourning, but because her abdomen and long legs are black.

The black widow is also known as the shoe-button spider because her glossy little abdomen looks like an old-fashioned shoe button.

The female golden-silk spider (*below, left*) weighs about 100 times more than the male. The male black widow spider (*below, right*) must be very careful when approaching the larger and more aggressive female.

like humans and many other animals, reproduce in one way only—sexually. Although there are a number of similarities in how these animals reproduce, each group has unique adaptations to ensure that reproduction is successful.

Courtship and Mating

In many spider species, males look different from females. They are smaller and have thinner legs. The female golden-silk spider is approximately 1 inch (2.5 centimeters) long and weighs 100 times as much as the male, whose body is 1/8 inch (0.3 centimeter) long. Some female orb-web spiders of tropical species may weigh as much as a thousand times more than their mates!

Male spiders are frequently much more colorful than females. The male of one species of purse-web spiders has a shiny black body and bright red legs, but the female is a dull brown. The male jumping lynx spider has a black abdomen with iridescent (rainbow-like) scales, but the female's abdomen is a pale gray. However, in nature there are always exceptions. The female golden-silk spider, for example, has beautiful silver, black, and gold markings, while the male is plain brown.

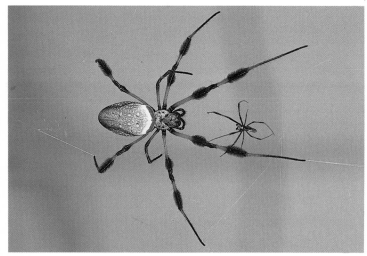

Another difference between adult female and male spiders is the design of their pedipalps—the small, leg-like appendages near the mouth. A male's pedipalps are enlarged at the tip and are especially designed to be used during mating.

When a male spider is ready to mate, he spins a sperm web and deposits a drop of liquid on the web. This liquid contains sperm produced in special glands in his abdomen. He transfers the drop of liquid from the web into cavities in the tips of his pedipalps—a process similar to putting liquid into an eyedropper.

Loaded up with sperm, the male starts looking for a female of his species. Males of some hunting species follow draglines laid down by females. Male orb weavers seem to search by touch, recognizing the feel of the silken threads woven by a female. For some species, perfumes produced by the females—or by their silk—may be sensed by special hairs on the males' legs.

Male spiders deposit their sperm on the tips of their pedipalps and then seek out females to mate. When a mate is found, the male inserts his sperm-dipped pedipalps into openings on the underside of the female's abdomen.

DID YOU KNOW

Mate Bait

Typically, spiders mate only once in their lives. To ensure survival of the species, it is very important for them to find mates. A female spider that is ready to mate may weave special perfumes into her web that are designed to attract males of the same species.

When a male arrives at the web, he doesn't want any competition from other males. Before he and the female mate, he rolls up her web, which prevents other males from sensing the perfume.

A female spider tends to regard anything that moves as a possible meal; therefore, a male has to be very careful about how he approaches her. Again, different species use different methods. A male orb weaver may announce his presence and desire to mate by gently pulling the threads of a female's web. A male jumping spider performs a courtship dance, waving his colorful legs to attract the female. A male nursery-web spider often brings the female a present: a juicy fly that he has caught.

After the female identifies the male as a member of her species and allows him to approach her, the two spiders mate. The male inserts one or both of his pedipalps into special openings on the underside of the female's abdomen. Sperm are then transferred from the pedipalps into seminal receptacles, pouches in the female's reproductive system.

As soon as mating is completed, the male leaves—before the female stops thinking of him as a mate and begins thinking of him as a meal.

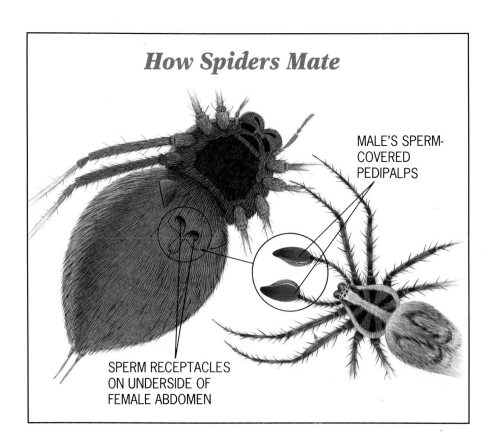

How Spiders Mate

MALE'S SPERM-COVERED PEDIPALPS

SPERM RECEPTACLES ON UNDERSIDE OF FEMALE ABDOMEN

Laying Eggs

After mating, the sperm is stored in the female's seminal receptacles for a week or even longer, until she begins to lay her eggs. As the eggs leave her body, they are fertilized by the sperm. That is, each egg unites with a sperm. The number of fertilized eggs laid by a female at one time varies with the species. Some little spiders lay only a few eggs. Average-size spiders lay about 200 eggs. Large tropical spiders may lay more than 2,000 eggs. The female protects the eggs by surrounding them with a case, or cocoon, made of a special kind of silk. Cocoons differ in size and shape, depending on the species.

Some spiders hide their egg cases on the undersides of rocks or plant leaves, then pay no more attention to them. The cases may be colored to blend in with the surroundings, making them difficult for predators to spot. One spider puts her egg case on a grass stem, then covers it with mud.

After laying their eggs, female spiders deposit them in a safe place. Some spiders, like the one at left above, hide their eggs on the undersides of rocks. Other spiders, like the one at right above, lay their eggs on a silk platform that is then enclosed and hidden.

DID YOU KNOW

Best-Laid Plans

Some spiders lay eggs no bigger than the period at the end of this sentence. But large tropical spiders may lay eggs the size of a pea. After an egg is laid, its outer layer hardens, which protects the developing organism inside and prevents it from drying out.

39

Reproduction and Growth

Some spiders, like this nursery-web spider, carry their egg cases around with them in order to ensure that their young are protected.

Other spiders will guard their egg cases until the eggs hatch. A European comb-footed spider keeps her egg case in a nest that she builds in the center of her web. If it gets too hot in the nest, she moves her egg case to a cooler spot on the web, then returns it to the nest when temperatures change again.

A spitting spider carries her egg case in her chelicerae until the eggs hatch and the babies can scatter in different directions. A nursery-web spider also holds her egg case in her chelicerae. These mothers cannot catch prey while they are carrying egg cases. Other species carry their egg cases between their legs, on their backs, or attached to their spinnerets. Carrying around an egg case can be awkward. A fisher spider has such a big egg case that she has to walk on tiptoe to keep from dragging the case on the ground.

Spiderlings

An egg contains food called yolk, which nourishes the developing spider until after it is born. The eggs of most spiders hatch in a few weeks, but some eggs laid in autumn do not hatch until the following spring. Other eggs laid in autumn hatch, but the newborn spiders stay inside the egg case until spring.

A newborn spider has no color, no hair, and no claws. It cannot eat or produce silk, so it depends on yolk that is still in its body. This tiny creature remains in the egg case until it sheds its exoskeleton and grows a new one.

Once they have their new exoskeleton, the babies are called spiderlings. They look a lot like their parents, but they are much smaller. They have color, hair, and claws, and they can spin silk. The baby spiders are also very hungry. Usually, a spiderling's first meal is one of its brothers or sisters!

As soon as they come out of the egg case, the surviving spiderlings begin spinning draglines. A short while later, they scatter in various directions by ballooning—letting the breeze carry them off to new homes, where there might not be so many other animals eager to eat them.

In species where the mother guards the egg case, she may also stay with the spiderlings for a while. She may protect the youngsters for a week or so, until they are old enough to look out for themselves.

Baby black widow spiders (*below, left*) crowd together in an open egg case. A female lynx spider (*below, right*) guards her spiderlings until they are old enough to be on their own.

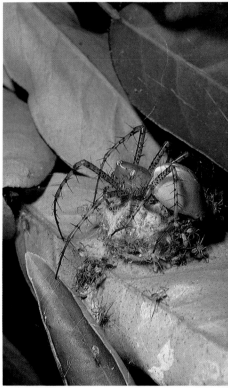

Molting and Growing

Unlike the skeleton inside your body, an exoskeleton cannot grow. Therefore, every so often a spider must shed its exoskeleton and grow a new one. This process is called molting. Spiders generally undergo 2 to 15 molts before becoming adults. Once they are adults, most spiders do not molt, although some female tarantulas, which have long lives, continue to molt once or twice a year.

Before molting, a spider stops eating. A web builder may hang upside down from its web. Other spiders may find a protected place where enemies are less likely to see them. During this period, a new exoskeleton begins to form under the old one. Some of the material from the old exoskeleton is broken

Get Off My Back

A female wolf spider is covered with her newborn young.

Like all male spiders, male wolf spiders disappear after mating. They do not help in caring for the eggs or spiderlings. But female wolf spiders are excellent mothers. After spinning a cocoon around her eggs, a female wolf spider attaches the cocoon to the spinnerets at the rear of her abdomen. She then drags the cocoon about wherever she goes.

After the eggs hatch, the mother wolf spider bites open the cocoon, and the spiderlings scamper out and climb onto her back. The newborn spiders grab hold of special hairs that are on the top of her abdomen and hold on tightly. If they didn't do this, they would fall off as their mother rushed about chasing prey or avoiding enemies. When the spiderlings are approximately a week old, they hop off their mother's back and leave her for good, ready to live on their own.

While a spiderling travels about on its mother's back, it may jump off for a quick drink of water, then climb up the mother's legs again. But the spiderling does not eat during this time. Some egg yolk remains in its body, which provides enough energy for the first days of the spiderling's life.

As their exoskeletons grow, spiders must shed their outer shells in order to make room for new ones. Here, a Honduran tarantula emerges from its freshly shed skin.

down by the spider's body and is used to make the new exoskeleton. This means that less building material has to come from stored food. It also thins the old exoskeleton, which becomes fragile and easier to tear.

Molting begins when the old exoskeleton splits along the sides of the body, and the spider slowly pulls itself out of the "shell." This is a tricky procedure. A wrong move may break a leg or cause the leg to become trapped inside the old exoskeleton.

For a while, the new exoskeleton is soft and flexible. The spider grows rapidly, stretching the exoskeleton before it dries and hardens.

Molting may take less than an hour for small spiders, but it takes much longer for tarantulas and other large spiders. Molting is a dangerous period for spiders because they are quite helpless during this time. Many animals, such as sowbugs and crickets, which do not attack spiders at other times, will prey on molting spiders. And, of course, the spiders' usual enemies, such as birds, find it much easier to catch spiders while they are molting.

Reproduction and Growth

5

Fitting into the Web of Life

Whatever areas spiders inhabit, they are part of a community of living things that includes many different kinds of plants and animals. Plants make their own food, but spiders and other animals cannot make food. To obtain the energy they need to survive, they must feed on something else. Many animals eat plants, and many other animals eat the animals that eat the plants. This flow of food and energy from one organism to another is called a food chain.

Eating...and Being Eaten

Spiders are important links in many food chains in their environment. They feed mainly on insects. Some of those insects ate leaves and other plant matter, and some ate insects that ate the plants. At some point, many insects become meals for spiders.

Opposite:
The beautiful patterns of an orb web are highlighted as dew glistens in the morning sun.

Some spiders, such as the North American black-and-yellow argiope, actually spin a special design into their webs in order to warn birds to steer clear. These spiders spin thick zigzag lines called stabilimenta, which are easy-to-see warning signs that keep birds from destroying webs by accidentally flying into them.

Spiders are also likely to become another animal's dinner. Frogs, toads, lizards, birds, and especially wasps commonly eat spiders. There are even some spiders that specialize in eating other spiders. These hunters are called pirate spiders. The ero spider is a pirate spider. It very quietly crawls onto the web of a comb-footed spider and tugs on some of the web threads, pretending it's an insect caught in the web. The host spider races over to attack, but ero is faster. It grabs the spider's leg and bites, injecting a deadly poison that kills the host spider within seconds.

A wasp that attacks spiders is the female tarantula hawk. She actually feeds on plant juices, but she attacks spiders so her babies will have food. After the wasp has mated and is ready to lay eggs, she hunts for a tarantula. She hopes to find a female, because female tarantulas are bigger and juicier than males. When she finds a tarantula, the female tarantula hawk stings the spider between its legs. While this paralyzes the tarantula, it doesn't kill it. Then the wasp digs a hole in the ground, drags the tarantula to the hole, and pushes it in. The wasp lays an egg on the body of the tarantula, then covers the hole with soil. When the newborn wasp hatches from the egg, it will feed on the paralyzed, but still living, tarantula. The young wasp eventually kills the helpless spider.

Defense in the Natural World

In order to survive, most living things have developed unique characteristics that give them advantages in the natural world. Sometimes these adaptations enable an organism to capture food in an effective way. Special adaptations also allow an organism to hide itself from other animals that want to eat it.

Spiders have many adaptations for catching food, meeting mates, and making sure their young will

A Typical Food Chain

A. Grass and other green plants make food.

B. A grasshopper eats the green plants.

C. The grasshopper is captured in the web of a spider and eaten.

D. The spider is eaten by a frog.

E. The frog is eaten by a heron.

F. When the heron dies, insects and bacteria feed on its decomposing body.

survive. They also have adaptations to protect themselves from their enemies. Having the ability to drop instantly on a dragline and being able to break off and lose a leg that is caught in an enemy's grip save many spiders.

The hairs on a spider's body are used not only as sense organs, but also as a means of defense. The hairy tarantula that lives in South American jungles uses some of these hairs as protection, much as a porcupine uses its quills to discourage its enemies. If it spots a mammal such as the pig-like peccary, the tarantula stands up on its back legs and rubs its front legs together to make a scary, hissing sound. If hissing doesn't make the animal run away, the tarantula brushes one of its back legs across a special patch of hairs on its abdomen. These hairs, which are armed

A Honduran tarantula uses its tiny hooked and barbed hairs to attack its enemies.

Spider Provider

Most spiders are solitary creatures. They live alone, except when they mate, and, perhaps, while caring for their young. If another spider enters their territory, they attack it.

A few species, however, form colonies. One is a tiny Mexican spider named *Mallos gregalis*. Thousands of these spiders live together in one big web, which may cover an entire tree! Ants are the favorite prey of these spiders. By working together, they can kill ants that are much bigger than any single spider could kill. Once an ant is caught, many spiders feed side by side on its body.

Another colonial spider that lives in Mexico is *Metepeira incrassata*. Each spider in this community weaves its own web in the grass, but it attaches the web to the webs of its neighbors. Sometimes a large field will be almost completely covered by these webs. An insect may be trapped when it lands on one web. But if the insect bounces off and escapes, it is likely to land on a neighboring web. By living close together in this way, these spiders need less energy for finding food.

Spiderwebs cover a field of reeds in a North American marsh.

DID YOU KNOW

Having a Ball

One species of spider actually pitches a sticky ball of glue at flying insects in order to capture prey. To trap moths, the bola spider first strings a line of silk from one web to another in order to support itself as it gets into position for the attack. Then the bola swings a special glue ball it has made from glands in its body. The spider whips the ball up at its target, hitting it about 50 percent of the time. Once a moth is stuck, it is reeled in by the spider and injected with poison for the final touch.

Many spiders protect themselves with skillful camouflage. The crab spider (*below, left*) can change its color to match the flower it is on. The mint spider, or Thomisus (*right*), mimics the color and the bristles of a mint plant to fool insects that land nearby.

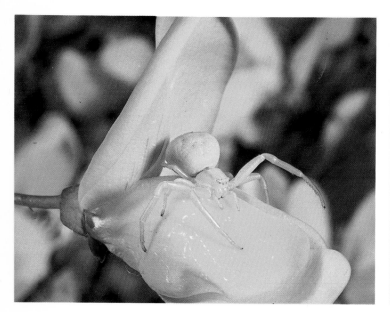

DID YOU KNOW

As Smooth as Silk

Because of its strength and flexibility, the silk spun by spiders can be used by these animals to protect their eggs, wrap up prey, and fly at altitudes of 25,000 feet (7,625 meters)! Some silk even reflects ultraviolet light to better attract insects. During their lifetimes, most spiders spin huge amounts of silk. Some webs would reach more than 300 miles (483 kilometers) if stretched out into one line!

with thousands of tiny hooks and barbs, break off easily. They enter the skin of the attacker's face and paws, where they cause a burning itch. Once a mammal experiences the pain caused by these hairs, it learns to stay away from hissing spiders.

Another protective adaptation that is used by many things in the natural world is camouflage—the ability to blend in with the surroundings. Crab spiders are masters of camouflage and can change their color to match their surroundings. For example, when the red-spotted crab spider, who lives in fields and meadows, visits goldenrod and other yellow flowers, its color changes to yellow. This makes the spider invisible to insects who visit the flowers—until they are caught in the spider's jaws, and it's too late for them to escape.

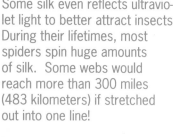

Mimicry is yet another kind of adaptation that is used as a defense. *Mimicry* means looking or acting like something else. Some spiders look like ants, and many predators avoid ants because ants produce bad-tasting chemicals. Since the spiders look like ants, their predators are fooled and do not eat the spiders.

Break a Leg

A large tropical hunting spider with a front leg missing.

Spiders have lots of enemies, but sometimes they are lucky. An enemy that grabs a spider by one of its legs may end up with the leg while the spider escapes. There is a weak point at one joint in each of the spider's legs. A leg can break off at this point without harm to the spider. A special mechanism seals the break so that no bleeding occurs.

In a young spider, the leg may actually grow back the next time the spider molts (sheds its exoskeleton). This doesn't happen in an adult spider—but since the adult still has seven legs, it can continue to function without much difficulty.

If a leg is torn off by an enemy, rather than separated at the weak point, the spider escapes with blood flowing out of its wound. Unless the spider acts quickly, it will bleed to death. The spider pulls at the injured leg with its other legs until it breaks off at the weak point, and the bleeding stops. Does the spider rush off, leaving the broken leg behind? Not necessarily. It may first suck out the juices from the leg.

Fitting into the Web of Life

Spiders and Humans: Together in the Natural World

Spiders are very important to humans. They eat enormous numbers of insects, including many that damage food crops, carry diseases, and harm us in other ways. In fact, scientists estimate that spiders eat more insects than all other kinds of insect-eating animals put together!

In spring and summer, when insects are most plentiful, spiders are also plentiful. More than 2 million spiders may live in 1 acre (0.4 hectare) of forest or grassland, and each of these spiders may catch an insect a day. This helps to limit the size of insect populations—the more insects that are killed by a spider, the fewer the number of insects that are left to reproduce more members of their species.

Some people are afraid of spiders. While it is true that many spiders will bite people, the venom of most spiders is effective only against the spiders' natural prey and is not harmful to humans. Also, the fangs of most species are too short or too fragile to break through human skin. Deaths from wasp and bee stings are much more common than deaths from spider bites.

About 3,000 species of spiders are found in the United States, but only 2 are truly dangerous to humans: the black widow and the brown recluse.

The body of the black widow is less than 1/2 inch (1.3 centimeter) long. Male black widows do not bite and are not dangerous to people. But the poison of an adult female causes an extremely painful bite—and may actually kill a person. The underside of the adult female's glossy black abdomen has red marks, often in the shape of an hourglass. The red marks are easy to see because these spiders hang upside down from their webs. Black widows build their webs under logs

Because spiders rely heavily on insects for food, they benefit humans by helping to control insect populations. Here, a crab spider eats a fly it has caught on a colorful yarrow blossom.

and fallen leaves. In houses, they build webs under furniture. Black widows seldom leave their webs, and if they are disturbed, they usually try to run away. But when a black widow is guarding her egg case, she will attack and bite anything that seems to threaten her precious eggs.

The brown recluse is about the same size as the black widow. Its cephalothorax is orange-yellow and is decorated with a dark violin-shaped marking. In warm places, brown recluses usually live outdoors, hiding under stones and in other secret places. In cooler habitats, they live in houses, where they hide in clothing or behind furniture. Several hours after a brown recluse bites a person, the skin around the wound turns red and begins to blister. In a few cases, the bite can cause severe illness or death. Even in less serious cases, the wound may take months to heal.

Other spiders that are known to be dangerous to humans include several South American species and a funnel-web spider that lives in Australia.

DID YOU KNOW

Not the Right Bite

People are not bitten by spiders very often. Much more common are bites from fleas, flies, bedbugs, ticks, and mites. These bites often are mistaken for spider bites. People who are bitten by a tiny creature should try to capture the animal. This will help a doctor determine what treatment is needed.

The brown recluse, like the black widow, is one of the more dangerous spiders for humans. Although its bite rarely causes death, it can cause illness and take months to heal.

Whey Out Spiders

Remember the nursery rhyme about Little Miss Muffet, who was frightened by a big spider while she was eating her curds and whey? This little girl was a real person named Patience Muffet who lived about 400 years ago.

Little Miss Muffet's father, Dr. Thomas Muffet, loved spiders. He thought that the webs they made in his home were beautiful. He also thought that spiders could cure all sorts of sicknesses. Whenever Miss Muffet was sick, her father would give her a medicine made from spiders. No wonder Miss Muffet was frightened by the little animals!

It is always advisable to see a doctor after being bitten by a spider, especially if the bite causes a rash or an illness. The doctor can prescribe medication to reduce pain, prevent infection, and fight other symptoms.

Protecting Spiders

The vast majority of spiders are helpful to humans because they eat pests. Too often, however, people kill these helpful little animals out of fear or just because they think spiders are "ugly."

Pesticides are often used to kill insect pests that destroy huge amounts of food raised by humans— food that could feed people around the world. But chemical pesticides do not kill pests only. They also harm other forms of life, including helpful spiders.

Killing spiders may actually result in bigger insect populations, since there will be fewer spiders around to kill the insects. In addition, since insects develop

The Silky Way

For many centuries, people have used spider silk to make pouches, fishing lines, and cross hairs in gunsights. In the 1700s, a Frenchman used spider silk to knit a few pairs of stockings. Today, researchers can collect silk from spiders by wrapping the end of a spider's silk strand on top of a motorized spindle. Each day, researchers can collect an average of more than 1,000 feet (305 meters) of silk from just one spider. But producing spider silk commercially is not yet practical. It still takes thousands of large, hardworking spiders to make enough silk for just one shirt.

Someday, however, it may be possible to buy a spider-silk shirt. Scientists are experimenting with spider genes, the blueprints in cells that determine an organism's characteristics. Scientists have located the genes that cause silk glands to produce silk, and they are now putting these genes into bacteria (kinds of one-celled organisms). They hope

this will cause the bacteria to produce the silk protein so the bacteria could be grown in large vats. The silk protein could then be removed from the vat and spun into thread. If this plan works, spider-silk shirts may become the hottest fashion items at your local mall!

An argiope wraps its prey in silk.

and reproduce more quickly than spiders, there will be many more insects around.

Instead of depending only on chemical pesticides to control insect pests, people can raise crops that are resistant to pests. We can also protect stored food by enclosing it in insect-proof containers. Above all, however, we can encourage the growth of the pests' natural enemies, including helpful insects and birds, as well as spiders. Nature, with its many food chains, has been doing this for millions of years.

DID YOU KNOW

Space Case

What do you think would happen to a spider's web-building skills in the weightless environment of outer space? The U.S. space agency decided to find out. It launched a spider into orbit. At first, the spider wove a badly shaped web. But in only three days, it had adapted to its new environment. It wove a web that looked just like the webs it weaves here on Earth.

Classification Chart of Spiders

Kingdom: Animal
Phylum: Arthropoda
Class: Arachnida
Order: Araneae

Scientists have identified about 35,000 species of spiders. These species are classified in about 70 families (different scientists use different classification systems). The following 17 families include the most common spiders.

Family	Common Members	Distinctive Features
Atypidae	purse-web spiders	build silk tubes camouflaged with bits of leaves and other debris
Ctenizidae	trap-door spiders	dig tunnel burrows with trapdoors; active at night
Dipluridae	sheet-web spiders	very long spinnerets; weave sheet webs with a funnel-like tube at one corner of the web
Theraphosidae	U.S. tarantulas, South American tarantulas, bird spiders	big and hairy; mostly live in burrows
Araneidae	orb-web spiders, argiopes, garden spiders	poor eyesight; many build orb webs
Ctenidae	wandering spiders	hunters; tropical and subtropical
Dinopidae	ogre-faced spiders	two of the eight eyes are very large; active at night
Linyphiidae	dwarf spiders, monkey spiders, sheet-web spiders	very small; most build sheet webs or dome-shaped webs

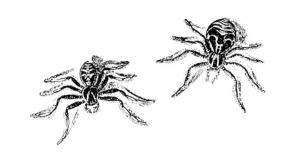

Family	Common Members	Distinctive Features
Lycosidae	wolf spiders, including European tarantulas	large; keen eyesight; excellent hunters that hunt mainly on the ground
Mimetidae	pirate spiders	small, slow-moving; enter webs of other spiders to prey on them
Oxyopidae	lynx spiders	sharp eyesight; excellent hunters that hunt mainly on plants; many are green
Pholcidae	daddy-longlegs spiders	small bodies and very long, thin legs; most with eight eyes, set close together
Pisauridae	fisher spiders	live near water and walk on it to hunt prey
Salticidae	jumping spiders	small and stout; large eyes; hunters; good jumpers
Scytodidae	spitting spiders	high carapace; six eyes; catch prey by spitting sticky glue at them
Theridiidae	comb-footed spiders, tangled-web spiders, widows	relatively small; often have a spherical abdomen; typically weave messy-looking webs
Thomisidae	crab spiders	move like crabs, with sideways scuttling movements; hunters that lie in wait for prey

THE ANIMAL KINGDOM

Porifera SPONGES

Cnidaria COELENTERATES

Platyhelminthes FLATWORMS

Nematoda ROUNDWORMS

Mollusca MOLLUSKS

Annelida TRUE WORMS

Hydrozoa HYDRAS, HYDROIDS

Scyphozoa JELLYFISH

Anthozoa SEA ANEMONES, CORALS

Turbellaria FREE-LIVING FLATWORMS

Monogenea PARASITIC FLUKES

Trematoda PARASITIC FLUKES

Cestoda TAPEWORMS

Polyplacophora CHITONS

Gastropoda SNAILS, SLUGS

Bivalvia CLAMS, SCALLOPS MUSSELS

Cephalopoda OCTOPUSES, SQUID

Polychaeta MARINE WORMS

Oligochaeta EARTHWORMS, FRESHWATER WORMS

Hirudinea LEECHES

Biological Classification

The branch of biology that deals with classification is called taxonomy, or systematics. Biological classification is the arrangement of living organisms into categories. Biologists have created a universal system of classification that they can share with one another, no matter where they study or what language they speak. The categories in a classification chart are based on the natural similarities of the organisms. The similarities considered are the structure of the organism, the development (reproduction and growth), biochemical and physiological functions (metabolism and senses), and evolutionary history. Biologists classify living things to show relationships between different groups of organisms, both ancient and modern. Classification charts are also useful in tracing the evolutionary pathways along which present-day organisms have evolved.

Over the years, the classification process has been altered as new information has become accepted. A long time ago, biologists used a two-kingdom system of classification; every living thing was considered a member of either the plant kingdom or the animal kingdom. Today, many biologists use a five-kingdom system that includes plants, animals, monera (microbes), protista (protozoa and certain molds), and fungi (non-green plants). In every kingdom, however, the hierarchy of classification remains the same. In this chart, groupings go from the most general categories (at the top) down to groups that are more and more specific. The most general grouping is PHYLUM. The most specific is ORDER. To use the chart, you may want to find the familiar name of an organism in a CLASS or ORDER box and then trace its classification upward until you reach its PHYLUM.

Insecta INSECTS

Chilopoda CENTIPEDES

Diplopoda MILLIPEDES

Symphyla, Pauropoda SYMPHYLANS, PAUROPODS

Collembola, SPRINGTAILS
Thysanura, SILVERFISH, BRISTLETAILS
Ephemeroptera, MAYFLIES
Odonata, DRAGONFLIES, DAMSELFLIES
Isoptera, TERMITES
Orthoptera, LOCUSTS, CRICKETS, GRASSHOPPERS
Dictyptera, COCKROACHES, MANTIDS
Dermaptera, EARWIGS
Phasmida, STICK INSECTS, LEAF INSECTS
Psocoptera, BOOK LICE, BARK LICE
Diplura, SIMPLE INSECTS
Protura, TELSONTAILS
Plecoptera, STONEFLIES
Grylloblattodea, TINY MOUNTAIN INSECTS
Strepsiptera, TWISTED-WINGED STYLOPIDS
Trichoptera, CADDIS FLIES

Embioptera, WEBSPINNERS
Thysanoptera, THRIPS
Mecoptera, SCORPION FLIES
Zoraptera, RARE TROPICAL INSECTS
Hemiptera, TRUE BUGS
Anoplura, SUCKING LICE
Mallophaga, BITING LICE, BIRD LICE
Homoptera, WHITE FLIES, APHIDS, SCALE INSECTS, CICADAS
Coleoptera, BEETLES, WEEVILS
Neuroptera, ALDERFLIES, LACEWINGS, ANT LIONS, SNAKE FLIES, DOBSONFLIES
Hymenoptera, ANTS, BEES, WASPS
Siphonaptera, FLEAS
Diptera, TRUE FLIES, MOSQUITOES, GNATS
Lepidoptera, BUTTERFLIES, MOTHS

Insectivora, INSECTIVORES (e.g., shrews, moles, hedgehogs)
Chiroptera, BATS
Dermoptera, FLYING LEMURS
Edentata, ANTEATERS, SLOTHS, ARMADILLOS
Pholidota, PANGOLINS
Primates, PROSIMIANS (e.g., lemurs, tarsiers, monkeys, apes, humans)
Rodentia, RODENTS (e.g., squirrels, rats, beavers, mice, porcupines)
Lagomorpha, RABBITS, HARES, PIKAS
Cetacea, WHALES, DOLPHINS, PORPOISES

Carnivora, CARNIVORES (e.g., cats, dogs, weasels, bears, hyenas)
Pinnipedia, SEALS, SEA LIONS, WALRUSES
Tubulidentata, AARDVARKS
Hyracoidea, HYRAXES
Proboscidea, ELEPHANTS
Sirenia, SEA COWS (e.g., manatees, dugongs)
Perissodactyla, ODD-TOED HOOFED MAMMALS (e.g., horses, rhinoceroses, tapirs)
Artiodactyla, EVEN-TOED HOOFED MAMMALS (e.g., hogs, cattle, camels, hippopotamuses)

58

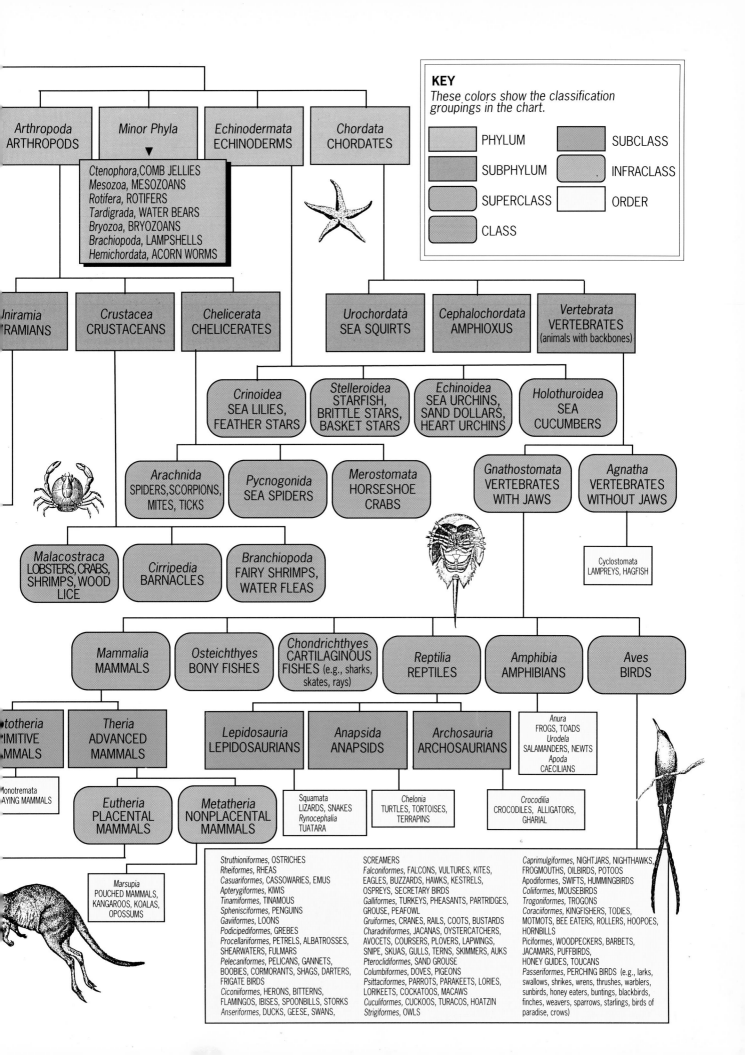

KEY
These colors show the classification groupings in the chart.

- PHYLUM
- SUBPHYLUM
- SUPERCLASS
- CLASS
- SUBCLASS
- INFRACLASS
- ORDER

Arthropoda ARTHROPODS

Minor Phyla ▼
- *Ctenophora*, COMB JELLIES
- *Mesozoa*, MESOZOANS
- *Rotifera*, ROTIFERS
- *Tardigrada*, WATER BEARS
- *Bryozoa*, BRYOZOANS
- *Brachiopoda*, LAMPSHELLS
- *Hemichordata*, ACORN WORMS

Echinodermata ECHINODERMS

Chordata CHORDATES

Uniramia UNIRAMIANS

Crustacea CRUSTACEANS

Chelicerata CHELICERATES

Urochordata SEA SQUIRTS

Cephalochordata AMPHIOXUS

Vertebrata VERTEBRATES (animals with backbones)

Crinoidea SEA LILIES, FEATHER STARS

Stelleroidea STARFISH, BRITTLE STARS, BASKET STARS

Echinoidea SEA URCHINS, SAND DOLLARS, HEART URCHINS

Holothuroidea SEA CUCUMBERS

Arachnida SPIDERS, SCORPIONS, MITES, TICKS

Pycnogonida SEA SPIDERS

Merostomata HORSESHOE CRABS

Gnathostomata VERTEBRATES WITH JAWS

Agnatha VERTEBRATES WITHOUT JAWS

Malacostraca LOBSTERS, CRABS, SHRIMPS, WOOD LICE

Cirripedia BARNACLES

Branchiopoda FAIRY SHRIMPS, WATER FLEAS

Cyclostomata LAMPREYS, HAGFISH

Mammalia MAMMALS

Osteichthyes BONY FISHES

Chondrichthyes CARTILAGINOUS FISHES (e.g., sharks, skates, rays)

Reptilia REPTILES

Amphibia AMPHIBIANS

Aves BIRDS

Prototheria PRIMITIVE MAMMALS

Theria ADVANCED MAMMALS

Lepidosauria LEPIDOSAURIANS

Anapsida ANAPSIDS

Archosauria ARCHOSAURIANS

Anura FROGS, TOADS
Urodela SALAMANDERS, NEWTS
Apoda CAECILIANS

Monotremata LAYING MAMMALS

Eutheria PLACENTAL MAMMALS

Metatheria NONPLACENTAL MAMMALS

Squamata LIZARDS, SNAKES
Rynocephalia TUATARA

Chelonia TURTLES, TORTOISES, TERRAPINS

Crocodilia CROCODILES, ALLIGATORS, GHARIAL

Marsupia POUCHED MAMMALS, KANGAROOS, KOALAS, OPOSSUMS

Struthioniformes, OSTRICHES
Rheiformes, RHEAS
Casuariformes, CASSOWARIES, EMUS
Apterygiformes, KIWIS
Tinamiformes, TINAMOUS
Sphenisciformes, PENGUINS
Gaviiformes, LOONS
Podicipediformes, GREBES
Procellariiformes, PETRELS, ALBATROSSES, SHEARWATERS, FULMARS
Pelecaniformes, PELICANS, GANNETS, BOOBIES, CORMORANTS, SHAGS, DARTERS, FRIGATE BIRDS
Ciconiiformes, HERONS, BITTERNS, FLAMINGOS, IBISES, SPOONBILLS, STORKS
Anseriformes, DUCKS, GEESE, SWANS,

SCREAMERS
Falconiformes, FALCONS, VULTURES, KITES, EAGLES, BUZZARDS, HAWKS, KESTRELS, OSPREYS, SECRETARY BIRDS
Galliformes, TURKEYS, PHEASANTS, PARTRIDGES, GROUSE, PEAFOWL
Gruiformes, CRANES, RAILS, COOTS, BUSTARDS
Charadriiformes, JACANAS, OYSTERCATCHERS, AVOCETS, COURSERS, PLOVERS, LAPWINGS, SNIPE, SKUAS, GULLS, TERNS, SKIMMERS, AUKS
Pteroclidiformes, SAND GROUSE
Columbiformes, DOVES, PIGEONS
Psittaciformes, PARROTS, PARAKEETS, LORIES, LORIKEETS, COCKATOOS, MACAWS
Cuculiformes, CUCKOOS, TURACOS, HOATZIN
Strigiformes, OWLS

Caprimulgiformes, NIGHTJARS, NIGHTHAWKS, FROGMOUTHS, OILBIRDS, POTOOS
Apodiformes, SWIFTS, HUMMINGBIRDS
Coliiformes, MOUSEBIRDS
Trogoniformes, TROGONS
Coraciiformes, KINGFISHERS, TODIES, MOTMOTS, BEE EATERS, ROLLERS, HOOPOES, HORNBILLS
Piciformes, WOODPECKERS, BARBETS, JACAMARS, PUFFBIRDS, HONEY GUIDES, TOUCANS
Passeriformes, PERCHING BIRDS (e.g., larks, swallows, shrikes, wrens, thrushes, warblers, sunbirds, honey eaters, buntings, blackbirds, finches, weavers, sparrows, starlings, birds of paradise, crows)

Glossary

abdomen The back part of a spider's body.

adaptation A body part or behavior that helps an organism survive in its environment.

appendage A body part attached to another body part.

arachnid A spider or one of its relatives, such as a scorpion, a tick, or a mite.

artery A blood vessel that carries blood from the heart to the body.

arthropod A segmented invertebrate with jointed legs and a tough outer skeleton.

asexual reproduction Reproduction that involves only one parent.

bacteria Kinds of one-celled organisms.

ballooning A method of travel used by young spiders; the breeze carries them from place to place.

book lungs One of two kinds of breathing organs found in spiders.

caeca Finger-shaped pouches attached to a spider's digestive tube where excess food is stored.

camouflage The colors, shapes, behaviors, or structures that enable an organism to blend with its surroundings.

carapace A large, tough shield that covers a spider's cephalothorax (head and thorax).

carnivore An organism that eats other animals.

cells The basic building blocks of organisms.

cephalothorax The front part of a spider's body, composed of the head and the thorax.

chelicerae The jaws of a spider; each chelicera ends in a fang.

coxal glands Glands that empty wastes through ducts that open between a spider's legs.

digestion The mechanical and chemical breakdown of food into substances the body can use for growth and energy.

dragline A double thread of silk formed by a spider during movement to serve as a safety line or to retrace a path.

evolve To change over a long period of time.

excretion The removal of bodily wastes.

exoskeleton The tough outer skeleton of a spider.

extinct No longer in existence.

fertilize To unite a sperm with an egg to create a new organism.

food chain The order in which a series of organisms feed on one another in an ecosystem.

fossil The preserved remains of a once-living thing.

genes The blueprints in cells that determine an organism's characteristics.

hemocyanin The chemical that carries oxygen throughout a spider's body.

hemoglobin The chemical in red blood cells that carries oxygen throughout the human body.

invertebrate An animal without a backbone.

lyriform organs Slit-like sense organs located in the exoskeleton of a spider.

Malpighian tubules Organs in a spider's abdomen that remove wastes from the blood.

membrane A thin layer of animal tissue.

metabolism The chemical processes in cells that are essential to life.

mimicry Looking or acting like something else.

molt To shed the exoskeleton.

pedipalp A small, leg-like appendage on each side of the spider's mouth.

pesticides Chemicals used to kill organisms that are considered harmful to humans.

predator An animal that kills other animals.

prey Animals that are eaten by other animals.

reproduction The process by which organisms create other members of their species.

seminal receptacles Pouches in a female spider's reproductive system where sperm are stored.

species A group of organisms that share many traits with one another and that can reproduce with one another.

sperm The male reproductive cell that fertilizes a female egg.

spiderling A baby spider.

spinnerets Finger-like appendages near the rear of a spider's abdomen, which spin silk produced by the silk glands.

tarsal organs Sensory structures located in the end segments of a spider's legs.

thorax The part of a spider's body joined to its head to form the cephalothorax, or front of its body.

tracheae Air-conveying tubes in the abdomen of a spider.

venom Poison.

vertebrate An animal with a backbone.

yolk Food in an egg that provides nourishment for the developing animal.

For Further Reading

Bailey, Donna. *What We Can Do About Protecting Nature*. New York: Franklin Watts, 1992.

Brown, Tom, Jr. *Tom Brown's Field Guide to Nature & Survival for Children*. New York: Berkley, 1989.

Burnie, David. *How Nature Works: One Hundred Ways Parents & Kids Can Share the Secrets of Nature*. New York: Reader's Digest Association, 1991.

Climo, Shirley. *Someone Saw a Spider: Spider Facts and Folktales*. New York: HarperCollins, 1985.

Collinson, Alan. *Grasslands*. New York: Dillon, 1992.

Dineen, Jacqueline. *Cotton & Silk*. Hillside: Enslow, 1988.

Goodman, Billy. *The Rain Forest*. New York: Little, Brown & Co., 1992.

Green, Carl R. and Sanford, William R. *The Tarantulas*. New York: Crestwood House, 1987.

Hopf, Alice. *Spiders*. New York: Dutton, 1990.

Julivert, Maria A. *Fascinating World of Spiders*. Hauppauge, NY: Barron, 1992.

La Bonte, Gail. *The Tarantula*. New York: Dillon, 1991.

Langone, John. *Our Endangered Earth: Our Fragile Environment & What We Can Do to Save It*. New York: Little, Brown & Co., 1992.

Lovett, Sarah. *Extremely Weird Spiders*. Santa Fe: John Muir, 1991.

Milne, Lorus J. *Insects and Spiders*. New York: Doubleday, 1992.

Nielsen, Nancy. *Black Widow Spider*. New York: Crestwood House, 1990.

Sabin, Francene. *Ecosystems and Food Chains*. Mahwah, NJ: Troll Associates, 1985.

Seidenberg, Steven. *Ecology and Conservation*. Milwaukee, WI: Gareth Stevens, 1990.

Wald, Mike. *What You Can Do for the Environment*. New York: Chelsea House, 1993.

Index

Photo Credits